Medium-sized,
Angled Wings

Medium-sized, Rounded Wings,
White or Yellow

Medium-sized,
Rounded Wings, Dark

Small, with Tails

Small, No Tails,
Thin-bodied

Small, No Tails, Thick-bodied

D0357293

Stokes Field Guides

Stokes Field Guide to Birds: Eastern Region

Stokes Field Guide to Birds: Western Region

Stokes Field Guide to Bird Songs: Eastern Region (CD/cassette)

Stokes Field Guide to Bird Songs: Western Region (CD/cassette)

Stokes Beginner's Guides

Stokes Beginner's Guide to Bats

Stokes Beginner's Guide to Birds: Eastern Region

Stokes Beginner's Guide to Birds: Western Region

Stokes Beginner's Guide to Butterflies

Stokes Beginner's Guide to Dragonflies

Stokes Beginner's Guide to Shorebirds

Stokes Backyard Nature Books

Stokes Bird Feeder Book

Stokes Bird Gardening Book

Stokes Birdhouse Book

Stokes Bluebird Book

Stokes Butterfly Book

Stokes Hummingbird Book

Stokes Oriole Book

Stokes Purple Martin Book

Stokes Wildflower Book: East of the Rockies

Stokes Wildflower Book: From the Rockies West

Stokes Nature Guides

Stokes Guide to Amphibians and Reptiles

Stokes Guide to Animal Tracking and Behavior

Stokes Guide to Bird Behavior, Volume 1

Stokes Guide to Bird Behavior, Volume 2

Stokes Guide to Bird Behavior, Volume 3

Stokes Guide to Enjoying Wildflowers

Stokes Guide to Nature in Winter

Stokes Guide to Observing Insect Lives

Other Stokes Books

The Natural History of Wild Shrubs and Vines

STOKES
Beginner's Guide
to Butterflies

Donald and Lillian Stokes *WITH* **Justin L. Brown**

Little, Brown and Company
Boston   New York   London

Copyright © 2001 by Donald W. Stokes and
Lillian Q. Stokes

All rights reserved. No part of this book may be
reproduced in any form or by any electronic or
mechanical means, including information storage
and retrieval systems, without permission in writ-
ing from the publisher, except by a reviewer who
may quote brief passages in a review.

First Edition

10 9 8 7 6 5 4 3 2 1

TWP-Sing

Library of Congress Cataloging-in-Publication Data

Stokes, Donald W.
    Stokes beginner's guide to butterflies / by
Donald and Lillian Stokes. — 1st ed.
        p.   cm.
    ISBN 0-316-81692-2
    1. Butterflies — Identification. 2. Butterflies —
North America — Identification. I. Title:
Beginner's guide to butterflies. II. Stokes,
Lillian Q. III. Title.

7-17-01

QL542 .S76 2001
595.78'9 — dc21   00-060636

Acknowledgment

We would like to thank Jane Ruffin for her
helpful suggestions and thoughtful review
of the photographs and text. Any errors that
may have slipped by are the sole responsi-
bility of the authors.

Printed in Singapore

Contents

How to Identify Butterflies

Welcome to *Stokes Beginner's Guide to Butterflies.* This is a user-friendly guide to identifying more than 100 of the most common and beautiful butterflies in North America.

Inside the front cover you will find eight categories of butterflies, each represented by an approximately life-sized silhouette and some text. Each category is connected to a color tab along the edge of the guide which leads to a section of the guide. To identify a butterfly, match it to the category it most closely resembles. Then turn to the color tab section of that category and flip through the pages to find your butterfly. Within the section, the butterflies will be grouped by color and other characteristics to further help you. In addition, inside the back cover

is an alphabetical index; this will help you quickly find a species for which you already know the name.

To summarize, there are three easy steps to identifying a butterfly you have seen:

1. Look at the size, shape, and color of your butterfly.
2. Choose the category inside the front cover that best matches your butterfly.
3. Turn to the color tab section of that category and flip through the pages to identify what you have seen.

Understanding the Eight Categories

The eight categories into which we have grouped the butterflies are designed to help you narrow your choices as you try to identify butterflies you have seen. They are just guidelines, for obviously the butterflies do not fit neatly into categories. Each category is represented by an approximately life-sized silhouette. When you are in the field, you can use your hand as a rough measuring stick to help you determine large, medium, and small in butterflies.

Large = The size of your fist.
Medium = The size of the space created by touching the tip of your middle finger to the tip of your thumb.

Small = The size of the outer joint of your thumb.

Here are further descriptions of the eight categories:

Large, with tails: These butterflies have tail-like projections off the back of their hindwings.

Large, no tails: These butterflies have rounded wings with no tails.

Medium-sized, angled wings: These butterflies have angular, jagged edges to the outer edge of their wings.

Medium-sized, rounded wings, white or yellow: These butterflies have rounded wings and are mostly white, yellow, or orange. They stand out because of their light colors and relatively little pattern on their wings.

Medium-sized, rounded wings, dark: These are basically all other medium-sized butterflies with rounded wings. Most are brownish, black, or have much patterning.

Small, with tails: These butterflies have minute, hairlike tails that can be a little hard to see but are distinctive. Occasionally, the tails may be broken off.

Small, no tails, thin-bodied: These are small butterflies with no tails. Their bodies are a fairly even thickness throughout and relatively thin.

Small, no tails, thick-bodied: These small butterflies belong to a group called skippers. They have a thick body, especially their middle section, and they fly rapidly. Some of the smaller ones, when at rest, hold their forewings and hindwings at different angles.

Understanding the Species Accounts

This guide is designed not only to help you identify butterflies but also to help you understand and enjoy their lives and behavior and to show you how to attract them to your backyard. Here is a brief description of the types of information given for each species.

Photographs — For the individual accounts, we have tried to illustrate the most common positions in which each butterfly is seen. For butterflies that rarely rest with their wings open, we have shown only the underside of the wings. This can be more helpful than you might think, for in many of these species their upper surfaces vary in color and pattern depending on the season and the sex of the butterfly, while their undersurfaces remain fairly constant.

For species that often rest with their wings open, we have shown the upper surfaces. In some cases, when it is especially important to identification, both the upper and undersides of the butterfly are shown.

The photographs were taken by many skilled photographers, and their names are listed in the photo credits on page 20.

Names — The common name of each butterfly is listed at the top of each account. Many butterfly names have changed over the last ten years, but these are the most recent and up-to-date common names according to the North American Butterfly Association checklist.

Beneath each common name is the scientific name of the species in italics.

The first word is the genus name, the second is the species name. Butterflies that are closely related have the same genus name.

Size — Following the names is the size of the butterfly in a range of inches. Butterflies can vary in size depending on their sex, the season of the brood, and the nutrition gotten by the larva.

Identification Description — These descriptions are designed to point out key identifying features of a species. We describe the "Above" and "Below" of each species (unless they are not distinctive). These are the upper and lower surfaces of the wings. Used with the photographs, the descriptions will help you identify the butterfly you have seen.

Habitat — This section describes the habitats where the butterfly is most often found. There can be quite a bit of variety, especially in the case of species using different habitats in the East and the West.

Adult Food — Most adult butterflies feed on nectar, but some feed on tree sap, fruit, and a variety of other foods as well. This information can also help you know what to offer a species to attract it to your backyard.

Larval Food — This is a list of the plants that caterpillars of this species eat. These plants are essential to the life of the butterflies. If you plant them, you can attract the egg-laying adult females to your yard and promote butterfly conservation.

Life History — This section gives you an idea of how long each stage in the life of a particular butterfly species takes. It is just an approximation, since many factors can affect the length of a given stage, such as weather, season, and latitude. The life stages are described in greater detail in the next section of this introduction.

Egg: This is the time spent in the egg stage.

Larva: This is the time it takes for the larva, or caterpillar, to grow and change into the pupa, or chrysalis.

Pupa: This is the time during which the caterpillar is transformed into an adult butterfly.

Adult: This is the amount of time the adult lives and is actively flying about.

Broods: This is the number of times this species completes its whole life cycle in one year. Since this can vary according to climate, we use N, S, E, and W to refer to northern, southern, eastern, and western portions of its North American range.

Overwinters: Since many butterflies become dormant in winter, this indicates the stage of their life cycle in which they spend their dormancy in winter. Some species are dormant in the North but may remain active all winter in the South. For a few species, it is not yet known how they spend the winter.

Range Maps — For each species there is a range map showing where that species can be found in North America. There is still a great deal of work to be done on learning the ranges of butterfly species, so these maps are only a rough guideline to help you out.

On the following pages of this introduction you will find information on butterfly life history, where to find butterflies, butterfly gardening and conservation, and other butterfly resources in books and on the Internet.

Butterflies Are Insects

Butterflies are a large group within the Class of insects. Insects are distinguished from other animals by having an external skeleton, three main sections to their bodies (head, thorax, and abdomen), and three pairs of legs all attached to their thorax, or middle body segment. In many cases, they also have two pairs of wings attached to their thorax.

Butterflies and moths both belong to the Order of insects called Lepidoptera, which means "scaled wings." Their wings are covered with fine dustlike scales that create all of the colors and patterns we so much enjoy. In general, butterflies are more colorful than moths. This is because they are active during the day and use color and sight to recognize their own species. Moths are mostly active at night and use primarily scent to locate and recognize mates.

The Life Stages of Butterflies

Butterflies have four different stages of their lives: egg, caterpillar (larva), chrysalis (pupa), and adult. All butterflies start as tiny eggs no bigger than the head of a pin. The eggs hatch and become tiny caterpillars that feed mostly on the leaves and flowers of plants. Some butterfly caterpillars secrete a sweet substance as a by-product of feeding, and this attracts ants that feed on the juices. It is a win-win situation; the ants get food and in turn protect the caterpillars from any insect enemies. As the caterpillars grow, they need to shed their skin because it is inelastic. Most species shed their skin four to six times before they are fully grown. This usually takes two to four weeks.

At this point they shed their larval skin for the last time and enter the next stage of their life. Underneath the larval skin is the pupal skin, which gradually hardens into a small case, usually oddly shaped. *Pupa* is the general term for this stage in insects; *chrysalis* is the specific term for this stage in butterflies. Inside the pupal case, the caterpillar is transforming into an adult butterfly with wings. This process can take from two weeks to several months.

When the adult is fully developed, it splits open the pupa and crawls out. While it hangs on to the shell of the pupa, it pumps fluid into the veins of the wings. When the wings are fully extended and hardened, it takes its first flight. The adult then feeds on nectar, fruit, and a variety of other foods, depending on the species. Males and females need to find each other and mate, and then the female lays her eggs. And the cycle continues.

A complete cycle, or generation, is called a brood, and butterfly species can go through from just one to as many as four or five broods per year, depending on the species and the number of warm months. Some species in the far South may remain active all year. But in areas where it gets cold, most species have to stop all activity, for no food is available. Each species usually has a fixed stage in which it overwinters, and its life cycle is synchronized with the seasons so that most members of a brood will have reached the proper stage when the weather turns cold. Some species, like Mourning Cloaks, spend the winter as adults hidden in protected places such as under bark or in a stone wall. Blues overwinter as pupae, and Viceroys overwinter as caterpillars. Very few butterflies are dormant in the egg stage.

Most adult butterflies live only about two weeks in the summer, but obviously if they are dormant as adults in winter, they can live much longer. Remember that the true length of a butterfly's life includes the four different stages — egg, caterpillar, chrysalis, and adult — altogether a minimum of about 2½ months.

Finding Butterflies

Certain places are better than others for finding butterflies. Butterflies are drawn to three kinds of habitats — where they can find food and other nutrients, where they can lay eggs, and where they can find mates.

Most adult butterflies drink nectar from flowers, so first look for butterflies around flowers. This includes gardens, roadsides, woods edges, and fields. Weedy roadsides can be quite good, even though some of the flowers may be small and inconspicuous. Any place where you see flowers growing can be a place to look for butterflies.

Some adult butterflies obtain food and nutrients from other sources.

Some go to the mud at the edges of puddles to get nutrients (this is called puddling), others may visit fruit that is starting to decay, some are attracted to sap oozing from trees, and a few are also attracted to animal droppings. These are all other places to look for butterflies.

Female butterflies lay their eggs on plants that the caterpillars will use as food when they hatch. Each species of butterfly usually has only a small number of larval food plants that it uses; these plants are called host species. If you know these plants, then you can go look for butterflies around them. For instance, Black Swallowtails lay their eggs on plants in the parsley family and Cabbage Whites lay their eggs on members of the cabbage family, so both these species may be found hovering around your vegetable garden looking to lay eggs. Some species lay their eggs on only one species of plant, making them more vulnerable to population declines if anything happens to that plant.

Butterflies also need to find mates. They do this in two main ways — perching and patrolling. A patrolling male butterfly will be found where females are feeding or laying eggs. It patrols back and forth and checks out every butterfly to see if it is a possible mate.

In perching, a male butterfly goes to an area where it is likely to encounter a female traveling along. These areas are often along paths, streams, or ridges. The male perches on vegetation or a rock or fallen log. It flies out to inspect passing butterflies to see if they are its own species. A variety of patrolling is called hilltopping. There are several species that make a point of going to hilltops to find mates. These include some of the swallowtails. Thus, you can also look for butterflies along paths, streams, and ridges and on open hilltops.

When to Look

Butterflies need to be warm to fly. They need to get their body temperature up to 85 to 100 degrees Fahrenheit in order to fly well. Thus, it is best to look for butterflies when the weather is warm and sunny, for this is when they will be active. On a cool, partly sunny day, the butterflies will fly about when the sun is out, but when a cloud comes by, they may stop because it is a little cooler.

Each species of butterfly has different times of year when the adults are active. One species may have a brood early and then not be seen for a month; and then when the next brood has matured, you will see adults again.

Because of this, and because of the different timetables the species are on, each week you go out you have a chance to see different species. In short, to see the most butterflies, go out on sunny days and continue to go out throughout the warm-weather months.

Equipment

A pair of binoculars that focus close-up, at about 6 feet away, is a great thing to have along when looking at butterflies. They enable you to see the butterflies' colors and markings in more detail. If your binoculars do not focus closely, you will find yourself having to back up to focus, thus making the image smaller. There are many brands of binoculars on the market that have close focus; they can be helpful for watching birds as well.

A still camera or a video camera — especially with zoom capability — is also nice to take out butterfly watching. In both cases, you can learn to carefully approach the butterflies to get a large picture. Then you can look even more carefully at your print, slide, or video to help you identify and enjoy what you saw.

People used to catch butterflies in large nets and then collect them. In today's world this is not done as much. We strongly encourage you not to collect butterflies but to let them continue flying and reproducing. However, you can still take a net out to briefly catch butterflies and then release them. This will enable you to look closely at the butterflies. But remember to catch them carefully so as not to damage them in any way; and try not to disturb egg-laying females, for they have a lot of important work to do.

A small journal can also be useful. We often make drawings of the butterflies that we see. This helps us remember their patterns, colors, and shapes. You can also make notes on where you saw the butterfly, what it was doing, what foods it was using, and when it was active.

In short, there are a tremendous variety of ways to enjoy butterflies.

How to Attract Butterflies

You can have the fun of attracting butterflies to your yard and helping them survive and reproduce by designing and planting a butterfly garden. First we will tell you the basic principles of a good butterfly garden; then we will show which are the best plants to use.

Nectar Plants

The first and most important part of a butterfly garden is lots of nectar-producing flowers. Most plants produce nectar, but some flowers are more favored by butterflies than others. Our top ten butterfly plants are listed later in this chapter.

Butterflies are attracted to the sight and smell of flowers, so it stands to reason that the more you have the better they will attract the butterflies. When buying plants, get several of each kind; then group these plants together into larger clumps.

Be sure to have flowers blooming throughout the entire warm season — in spring, summer, fall, and even winter if you are in the South. This ensures that your butterflies will always have food.

It is also good to have plants of various heights, since different species sometimes feed at different heights. So place tall flowering plants at the back of your garden, medium-sized plants in the middle, and small plants in the front. It is also good to leave lots of room around your flowering plants, especially the taller ones, so that butterflies can easily get to the blossoms.

Food for Caterpillars

A butterfly garden can attract feeding adults, but it can also attract egg-laying females. When you do this, you are helping butterflies grow and reproduce — you are a part of butterfly conservation.

The plants that females lay their eggs on are called larval food plants or host plants, because the caterpillars eat the leaves and sometimes the flowers. This may seem to be at odds with your efforts to grow plants and not have them eaten, but there are ways to accommodate the caterpillars and your aesthetic sense.

Some people put their larval food plants in a separate garden. This can be good since some of these plants are considered weeds, wildflowers, or grasses. Other gardeners grow enough plants so the caterpillars can feed without hurting the look of the garden. Sometimes we grow larval food plants in containers that can be moved around and to the back of the garden if they begin to look a little scraggly. In all cases, the excitement of finding eggs on your plants and then watching the caterpillars grow is hard to match. Some of the easiest and best larval food plants are listed later in this chapter.

Have Lots of Sun

Butterflies need warmth to keep active. This means lots of sun. Sunshine and warmth enable butterflies to be active for more hours each day. They can start feeding earlier and keep feeding later. Males can spend more time courting females, and females can continue laying eggs for more of the day. In addition, the warmth helps the caterpillars keep actively eating for longer periods and thus helps them develop faster. The sun also encourages larval plants to grow more leaves faster. Thus, sun is extremely important in a butterfly garden.

When butterflies get cool, they do something called basking. To bask, they perch on open spots and hold their wings perpendicular to the sun's rays. Absorbing the warmth with their wings and body helps them fly about sooner on a cool day. Provide some basking places for the butterflies in your garden. An exposed rock on the ground or some dark evergreens facing the sun can be good basking spots for butterflies.

Shelter

Shelter from the wind is also important to butterflies. Winds buffet them about, making them expend added energy as they try to fly and go about their lives. Winds also can make a habitat cooler and inhibit butterfly activity.

Try to create some shelter from the wind by having a hedge of shrubs or trees around your garden, especially protecting it from the prevailing winds. A fence or rock wall can also provide protection from the wind.

Top Ten Nectar Plants for Butterflies

Here are our recommendations for ten super plants from which butterflies love to take nectar. All are available from nurseries or plant mail-order catalogs.

Black-eyed Susan (*Rudbeckia* spp.)
This is also called gloriosa daisy and grows about 3 feet high. One of our favorite species is *Rudbeckia fulgida* 'Goldstrum.' Pearl Crescents love this plant.

Joe-Pye Weed (*Eupatorium* spp.)
This grows 5 to 9 feet tall and is a native wildflower. There are increasingly more varieties available in nurseries. One large-flowered variety is called 'Gateway.'

Aster (*Aster* spp.)
Asters are sometimes called Michaelmas daisies and grow 3 to 5 feet tall. Our favorite is the wildflower called New England aster. A cultivated variety is called 'September Ruby.' These plants often bloom late in fall and provide nectar for butterflies late in the season.

Butterfly Weed (*Asclepias tuberosa*)
This is a type of milkweed that is very attractive to butterflies. Other species of milkweeds will also be good for butterflies. This species grows 2 to 3 feet tall and prefers dry sandy soil.

Coreopsis (*Coreopsis* spp.)
There are many species of this lovely yellow-flowered plant, which blooms throughout the summer. It is slightly shorter than some of the other top ten, growing to about 2 feet tall.

Pentas (*Pentas lanceolata*)
This great butterfly plant is a perennial in the deep South but must be grown as an annual or overwintered in a greenhouse farther north. It grows about 1½ feet in height.

Liatris (*Liatris* spp.)
Also called blazing star or gay-feather, liatris grows to 2 to 4 feet. Its long spikes of usually purple flowers are both beautiful in the garden and very attractive to butterflies.

Butterfly Bush (*Buddleia* spp.)
This shrub is perhaps our favorite butterfly plant. In northern zones it may die to the ground in winter but come back in spring; it is hardy farther south. Long clusters of fragrant flowers really get the butterflies to stop and visit. It comes in a variety of colors,

including purple, white, and pink, and reaches 6 to 15 feet in height.

Lantana (*Lantana* spp.)
This sprawling plant grows 1 to 3 feet tall and is wonderful for the front of a border. It is grown as a perennial in the South but is an annual in the North.

Purple Coneflower (*Echinacea purpurea*)
This looks like a pink version of black-eyed Susan. Butterflies really stay on it for long periods as they feed. Grows 2 to 3 feet tall and is a perennial. Also comes in a white version with yellow centers.

The more of these plants you grow in your garden, the better chance you have of attracting butterflies. There are many other species of good butterfly plants. For a complete list, see the *Stokes Butterfly Book*.

A Few Good Larval Food Plants

There are many larval food plants for our common butterflies. In some cases, a butterfly species may lay its eggs on only one species of plant; in other cases, a butterfly may be more of a generalist, laying its eggs on any member of a whole family of plants or on several species from a variety of plant families.

Below is a list of some of the more common larval food plants that host several species of butterflies. Next to them are the butterflies that lay their eggs on them.

Trees and Shrubs

Aspen — White Admiral, Red-spotted Purple, Western Admiral, Lorquin's Admiral, Viceroy, Mourning Cloak, Tiger Swallowtail, Western Tiger Swallowtail

Cherry — Red-spotted Purple, Tiger Swallowtail, Spring Azure

Citrus Trees — Anise Swallowtail, Giant Swallowtail

Elm — Comma, Question Mark, Mourning Cloak

Hackberry — Question Mark, Comma, Hackberry Emperor, Tawny Emperor, American Snout, Mourning Cloak

Spicebush — Spicebush Swallowtail

Willow — Western Admiral, Lorquin's Admiral, Viceroy, Mourning Cloak, Western Tiger Swallowtail

(*continued*)

Wildflowers, Flowers, Vegetables

Alfalfa — Clouded Sulphur, Orange Sulphur, Eastern Tailed-Blue

Cabbage Family — Cabbage White, Checkered White

Clover — Clouded Sulphur, Orange Sulphur, Eastern Tailed-Blue

False Nettle — Red Admiral, Question Mark, Comma, Milbert's Tortoiseshell

Mallow — West Coast Lady, Gray Hairstreak

Milk Vetch — Western Tailed-Blue and other blues

Milkweed — Monarch, Queen

Nettle — Red Admiral, Question Mark, Comma, Milbert's Tortoiseshell

Queen Anne's Lace and Parsley — Black Swallowtail, Anise Swallowtail

Sorrel, Dock — American Copper, Purplish Copper

Vetch — Orange Sulphur, Eastern Tailed-Blue, Western Tailed-Blue, other blues

Violet — Great Spangled Fritillary, Meadow Fritillary, other fritillaries

Winter Cress — Sara Orangetip, Falcate Orangetip, Cabbage White

Resources

Books

Here are two other books we wrote that we think you will find enjoyable in helping you attract and understand butterflies.

Stokes Butterfly Book. Boston: Little, Brown and Company, 1991. This book tells you all you need to make a wonderful butterfly garden and also describes the life history and behavior of the different species. It includes nearly 150 photographs of butterflies in all their life stages. A must for any butterfly lover.

Stokes Guide to Observing Insect Lives. Boston: Little, Brown and Company, 1983. This is a guide for the overall insect enthusiast. It includes fascinating information about some of the most obvious insects you encounter, from butterflies to fireflies to dragonflies.

Resources on the Internet

The best way to access the greatest number of resources is to go to the Internet. On the Internet you can learn about books, public gardens, butterfly houses, butterfly societies, butterfly ranges, butterfly research, butterfly gardening, and much more. Here are a few good Web sites that will in turn link you to many other excellent sites.

Butterflies of North America

www.npwrc.usgs.gov/resource/distr/lepid/bflyusa/bflyusa.htm

Children's Butterfly Site

www.mesc.usgs.gov/butterfly/butterfly.html

Electronic Resources on Lepidoptera

www.chebucto.ns.ca./Environment/NHR/lepidoptera.html

North American Butterfly Association

www.naba.org/

The Butterfly Web Site

www.mgfx.com/butterfly/
Within this site: Butterfly Public Gardens and Butterfly Houses
www.butterflywebsite.com/Gardens/index.cfm#usa

The Lepidopterists' Society

www.furman.edu/~snyder/snyder/lep/

Photo Credits

The majority of the butterflies shown were photographed in the wild in their natural habitat. Others were reared for study and then photographed.

The letter *i* following a page number refers to a smaller picture inset within the main picture.

Jim Brock: 24, 48
Herbert Clarke: 61, 61i, 82, 87, 90, 93, 94, 118
Raymond Coleman: 28i, 38i
Bruce Flaig: 78, 78i
Clair Postmus: 26, 26i, 28, 30, 55, 55i, 56
Jane Ruffin: 23, 23i, 25, 29, 30i, 31, 31i, 32, 33, 34, 35, 36i, 37, 37i, 38, 39, 39i, 41, 45, 47, 52, 53i, 57, 57i, 58, 59, 59i, 60, 60i, 66, 67, 68, 70, 73, 75i, 77i, 79, 79i, 83, 85, 86, 88, 91, 92, 97, 99, 100, 101, 102, 103, 103i, 109, 109i, 110i, 111, 115, 117, 119, 121, 122, 125, 125i
Larry Sansone: 110, 113
John Shaw: 27, 71, 107
Pat Sutton: 36, 70i
John Tveten: 35i, 40, 40i, 42, 42i, 43, 44, 46, 49, 50, 51, 53, 54, 62, 62i, 63, 63i, 64, 64i, 65, 65i, 68i, 69, 69i, 72, 74, 75, 76, 76i, 77, 80, 81, 84, 89, 95, 96, 98, 98i, 102i, 104, 105, 106, 108, 112, 114, 116, 120, 123, 123i, 124, 126, 126i, 127, 128

Identification

Habitat

Adult Food

Larval Food

Life History

Identification Pages

Eastern Tiger Swallowtail
Papilio glaucus, 3⅛–5½"

I.D. Large, with tails. ABOVE AND BELOW: Yellow with black stripes. Some females are dark with single row of yellow even-sized spots on the trailing edge of the forewing.
• Distinguished from Western Tiger Swallowtail by range.

Habitat Gardens, meadows, edge habitats.

Adult Food Nectar, puddling.

Larval Food N: aspens; S: black cherry, tulip tree, sweet bay.

Life History Egg: 4–10 days; Larva: 3–4 weeks; Pupa: 10–20 days; Adult: 6–14 days. Broods: N: 2; S: 3. Overwinters as pupa.

Western Tiger Swallowtail
Papilio rutulus, 2¾ – 3⅞"

I.D.
Large, with tails. ABOVE AND BELOW: Yellow with black stripes. • Distinguished from Eastern Tiger Swallowtail by range.

Habitat
Gardens, meadows, edge habitats.

Adult Food
Nectar, puddling.

Larval Food
Aspens, poplars, willows, alders, ashes.

Life History
Egg: 4–10 days; Larva: 3–4 weeks; Pupa: 10–20 days; Adult: 6–14 days. Broods: N: 2; S: 3. Overwinters as pupa.

Two-tailed Swallowtail
Papilio multicaudata, 3⅜–5⅛"

I.D.
Large, with two tails on each hindwing, the outer one longer than the inner one. ABOVE AND BELOW: Yellow with black stripes.

Habitat
Semiarid areas.

Adult Food
Nectar, puddling.

Larval Food
Willow, cherry, poplar, ash.

Life History
Egg: 4–10 days; Larva: 3–4 weeks; Pupa: 10–20 days; Adult: 6–14 days. Broods: N: 1; S: 2+. Overwinters as pupa.

Giant Swallowtail

Papilio cresphontes, 3⅜–5½″

I.D.

Large, with tails. ABOVE: Forewings dark with wide yellow band going across the butterfly from wing tip to wing tip; tips of tails have yellow spots. BELOW: Mostly pale yellow.

Habitat

Open areas, citrus groves.

Adult Food

Nectar, dung, puddling.

Larval Food

Prickly ash, hop tree, citrus trees.

Life History

Egg: 4–10 days; Larva: 3–4 weeks; Pupa: 10–20 days; Adult: 6–14 days. Broods: N: 2; S: 2–3. Overwinters as pupa.

Anise Swallowtail
Papilio zelicaon, 2⅝–3″

I.D.

Large, with tails. ABOVE: Black with yellow dots along wing margins. Forewing has large band of yellow through center.

Habitat

Varied.

Adult Food

Nectar, puddling.

Larval Food

Sweet fennel, biscuit root, citrus trees.

Life History

Egg: 4–10 days; Larva: 3–4 weeks; Pupa: 10–20 days; Adult: 6–14 days. Broods: N: 1; S: 3. Overwinters as pupa.

Black Swallowtail
Papilio polyxenes, 2⅝ – 3½"

I.D. Large, with tails. ABOVE: Wings black with two rows of yellow spots along edge, more pronounced in male than female. Hindwings have iridescent blue between rows of yellow spots. BELOW: Hindwings have two rows of orange spots.

Habitat Varied open areas, gardens, parks.

Adult Food Nectar, puddling.

Larval Food Wild carrot, dill, parsley, parsnip.

Life History Egg: 4–10 days; Larva: 3–4 weeks; Pupa: 10–20 days; Adult: 6–14 days. Broods: N: 2; S: 3. Overwinters as pupa.

Palamedes Swallowtail
Papilio palamedes, 3⅛–5½"

I.D. Very large, with tails. ABOVE: Dark wings with yellow spots. Hindwings have solid yellow band across center.

Habitat Coastal wetlands, swamps.

Adult Food Nectar, puddling.

Larval Food Red bay.

Life History Egg: 4–10 days; Larva: 3–4 weeks; Pupa: 10–20 days; Adult: 6–14 days. Broods: N: 2; S: 2–3. Overwinters as pupa and possibly larva.

29

Spicebush Swallowtail

Papilio troilus, 3½ – 4½"

I.D.

Large butterfly, with tails. ABOVE: Dark wings with single row of whitish dots along margin which decrease in size toward tip. BELOW: Hindwing has two rows of large orange dots.

Habitat

Open woods, habitat edges.

Adult Food

Nectar, puddling.

Larval Food

Sassafras, spicebush.

Life History

Egg: 4–10 days; Larva: 3–4 weeks; Pupa: 10–20 days; Adult: 6–14 days. Broods: N: 2; S: 3. Overwinters as pupa.

Pipevine Swallowtail
Battus philenor, 2³⁄₄ – 3³⁄₈″

I.D.
Large, with tails. ABOVE: Forewings black, relatively unmarked; hindwings iridescent blue with small white dots across the interior. BELOW: Hindwings have single row of large orange spots along leading edge.

Habitat
Open areas, woods edges, gardens.

Adult Food
Nectar, puddling.

Larval Food
Pipevines.

Life History
Egg: 4–10 days; Larva: 3–4 weeks; Pupa: 10–20 days; Adult: 6–14 days. Broods: N: 2; S: 4. Overwinters as pupa.

Zebra Swallowtail
Eurytides marcellus, 2³⁄₈–3¹⁄₂″

I.D.

Large, with tails; tails long. ABOVE: Whitish with black stripes. BELOW: Similar; hindwing has red stripe through middle.

Habitat

Brushy areas, often near water.

Adult Food

Nectar, puddling.

Larval Food

Pawpaw.

Life History

Egg: 4–10 days; Larva: 3–4 weeks; Pupa: 10–20 days; Adult: 6–14 days. Broods: N: 1; S: 4. Overwinters as pupa.

Monarch
Danaus plexippus, 3½–4″

I.D.
Large, no tails. ABOVE AND BELOW: Orange with black lined veins; black border with small white spots; hindwings have no horizontal bar crossing the veins (as in Viceroy).

Habitat
Wide variety of open habitats, fields, gardens, coasts.

Adult Food
Nectar.

Larval Food
Milkweeds.

Life History
Egg: 4–6 days; Larva: 2–3 weeks; Pupa: 5–15 days; Adult: 1–3 months. Broods: N: 1–4; S: 4–6. Overwinters as adult.

Queen
Danaus gilippus, 3–3⅜"

I.D. Large, no tails. ABOVE: Dark orange with a black border; small white spots on outer half of forewings. BELOW: Similar, with veins marked with black.

Habitat Meadows, fields, woods edges, gardens.

Adult Food Nectar.

Larval Food Milkweeds.

Life History Egg: 4–6 days; Larva: 2–3 weeks; Pupa: 5–15 days; Adult: 1–3 months. Broods: N: 1; S: 4+. Overwinters as adult.

Great Spangled Fritillary
Speyeria cybele, 2⅛ – 3″

I.D.

Large, no tails. ABOVE: Wings orange checkered with black; no solid dark border on either wing. BELOW: Hindwing has wide dark margin bordered by silver spots and a wide band of pale brown; many large silver spots on interior.

Habitat

Moist open areas, including meadows, gardens, pastures, paths.

Adult Food

Nectar.

Larval Food

Violets.

Life History

Egg: 10–15 days; Larva: overwinters; Pupa: 14–24 days; Adult: 2–10 weeks. Broods: 1. Overwinters as larva.

Regal Fritillary
Speyeria idalia, 2⅝–3⅝"

I.D. Large, no tails. ABOVE: Wings orange checkered with black; forewing has white-spotted black border. Hindwing black with two rows of white dots. BELOW: Hindwing olive brown with large silver spots.

Habitat Moist open areas and tall-grass prairies.

Adult Food Nectar.

Larval Food Violets.

Life History Egg: 10–15 days; Larva: overwinters; Pupa: 14–24 days; Adult: 2–10 weeks. Broods: 1. Overwinters as larva.

Question Mark
Polygonia interrogationis, 2³/₈ – 2⁵/₈"

I.D. Medium-sized, angled wings. ABOVE: Orange with black spots. Note strongly hooked shape to tip of forewing. Tails vary from short to long. BELOW: Hindwing has a silver comma plus a dot, the "question mark."

Habitat Open wooded areas, woods edges.

Adult Food Sap, carrion, fruit, dung, puddling.

Larval Food Elms, hackberry, hops, nettles.

Life History Egg: 4–14 days; Larva: 3–4 weeks; Pupa: 7–18 days; Adult: 6–20 days. Broods: N: 2; S: 4. Overwinters as adult.

Eastern Comma
Polygonia comma, 1¾–2″

I.D.
Medium-sized, angled wings. Above: Orange with black markings. Note wing tips not strongly recurved into a hook. Tails short. Below: Hindwing has silver "comma."

Habitat
Deciduous woods, marshes, swamps.

Adult Food
Sap, carrion, fruit, dung.

Larval Food
Hops, nettles, elms.

Life History
Egg: 4–14 days; Larva: 3–4 weeks; Pupa: 7–18 days; Adult: 6–20 days. Broods: 2. Overwinters as adult.

Green Comma
Polygonia faunus, 1⅞–2″

I.D. Medium-sized, angled wings. Very jagged wing edges. ABOVE: Wings orange with wide black border. BELOW: Thin greenish lines or spots along the jagged border; hindwing has silver "comma."

Habitat Coniferous forests, woods openings, canyons.

Adult Food Nectar, dung, carrion.

Larval Food Willows, birches, alders.

Life History Egg: 4–14 days; Larva: 3–4 weeks; Pupa: 7–18 days; Adult: 6–20 days. Broods: 1. Overwinters as adult.

Milbert's Tortoiseshell
Nymphalis milberti, 1¾ – 2″

I.D.

Medium-sized, angled wings. ABOVE: Wings dark with wide orange to yellow band along thin black border. BELOW: Dark with wide pale band near margin.

Habitat

Moist woodlands, meadows.

Adult Food

Nectar, some sap and fruit.

Larval Food

Nettles.

Life History

Egg: 4–14 days; Larva: 3–4 weeks; Pupa: 7–18 days; Adult: 6–20 days. Broods: N: 1; S: 2. Overwinters as adult.

Mourning Cloak
Nymphalis antiopa, 2⁷/₈ – 3³/₈″

I.D.

Medium-sized, angled wings. ABOVE AND BELOW: Dark with speckled yellow border.

Habitat

Varied habitats with trees.

Adult Food

Sap, fruit, nectar, puddling.

Larval Food

Willows, aspens, elms, birches, hackberry.

Life History

Egg: 4–14 days; Larva: 3–4 weeks; Pupa: 7–18 days; Adult: 6–20 days. Broods: 1–2. Overwinters as adult.

American Snout

Libytheana carinenta, 1⅝–1⅞"

I.D.
Medium-sized, angled wings. Long pointed "snout." ABOVE: Brown with orange patches and white dots. BELOW: Forewing orange at base with white patch on margin.

Habitat
Woods edges, thorn scrub, areas with hackberry.

Adult Food
Nectar, rotting fruit, puddling.

Larval Food
Hackberry.

Life History
Egg: 4–8 days?; Larva: 2–3 weeks?; Pupa: 7–14 days?; Adult: 4–12 days. Broods: N: 2; S: 2–4. Overwinters as adult.

Goatweed Leafwing
Anaea andria, 2⅜ – 3"

I.D.
Medium-sized, angled wings. ABOVE: Orange to brownish orange above with darker border; forewing sharply pointed at tip; hindwing with short tail. BELOW: Looks just like a dried leaf.

Habitat
Open woods and edge habitats.

Adult Food
Sap, rotting fruit, dung, bird droppings.

Larval Food
Goatweeds and other crotons.

Life History
Egg: 3–9 days; Larva: 4–6 weeks; Pupa: 7–10 days; Adult: 6–14 days. Broods: 2–4. Overwinters as adult.

Mustard White

Pieris napi, 1½–1⅝"

I.D. Medium-sized, rounded wings, white. ABOVE: Variable; white, usually without any other markings. BELOW: Cream-colored, usually with darker veins.

Habitat Deciduous forests, habitat edges.

Adult Food Nectar.

Larval Food Mustards, rock cress, toothwort, watercress.

Life History Egg: 4–7 days; Larva: 2–4 weeks; Pupa: 8–14 days; Adult: 6–10 days. Broods: N: 1; S: 2–3. Overwinters as pupa.

Cabbage White
Pieris rapae, 1¼–1⅞"

I.D.

Medium-sized, rounded wings, white. ABOVE: Forewings have dark tips and one or two interior spots (one in male and two in female). BELOW: Yellow on hindwing and tip of forewing contrasts with white on rest of forewing.

Habitat

Fields, gardens, weedy lots.

Adult Food

Nectar, rarely puddling.

Larval Food

Mustards, especially cabbage, broccoli.

Life History

Egg: 4–7 days; Larva: 2–4 weeks; Pupa: 8–14 days; Adult: 6–10 days. Broods: N: 2; S: 3+. Overwinters as pupa.

Great Southern White
Ascia monuste, 1¾–2¼″

I.D.

Medium-sized, rounded wings, white. ABOVE: Forewing white with some charcoal along edges. Hindwing all white. BELOW: All white in male (left); all white to grayish markings on veins in female (right). Antennae have blue tips.

Habitat

Sandy coastal plains and islands.

Adult Food

Nectar.

Larval Food

Beach cabbage, saltwort, mustards.

Life History

Egg: 4–7 days; Larva: 2–4 weeks; Pupa: 8–14 days; Adult: 6–10 days. Broods: 3+. Active throughout the year.

Checkered White

Pontia protodice, 1¼–1¾"

I.D.

Medium-sized, rounded wings, white. ABOVE: White butterfly with many dark patches on forewings. More dark patches on females and spring broods. BELOW: Veins heavily outlined with brown or olive; dark rectangular patch on front edge of forewing.

Habitat

Mostly low-elevation fields and weedy areas.

Adult Food

Nectar.

Larval Food

Mustards.

Life History

Egg: 4–7 days; Larva: 2–4 weeks; Pupa: 8–14 days; Adult: 6–10 days. Broods: N: 3; S: 3+. Overwinters as pupa.

Sara Orangetip
Anthocharis sara, 1¼–1¾"

I.D. Medium-sized, rounded wings, white. ABOVE AND BELOW: Tips of forewings rounded and with orange, brighter above than below. BELOW: Hindwings mottled greenish.

Habitat Varied open sunny habitats.

Adult Food Nectar.

Larval Food Mustards.

Life History Egg: 4–7 days; Larva: 2–4 weeks; Pupa: 8–14 days; Adult: 6–10 days. Broods: E: 1; W: 2. Overwinters as pupa.

Falcate Orangetip

Anthocharis midea, 1³/₈ – 1½"

I.D.

Medium-sized, forewings pointed at tip, white. ABOVE: Forewing white with single interior black spot and black-and-white-checkered edge. Male has orange wing tip, female has white wing tip. BELOW: Heavily mottled and no orange spot (compare Sara Orangetip, opposite).

Habitat

Open woodlands.

Adult Food

Nectar.

Larval Food

Mustards.

Life History

Egg: 4–7 days; Larva: 2–4 weeks; Pupa: 8–14 days; Adult: 6–10 days. Broods: 1. Overwinters as pupa.

49

Clouded Sulphur
Colias philodice, 1½–2"

I.D.

Medium-sized, rounded wings, yellow. ABOVE: Wings yellow to greenish yellow, bordered with black. BELOW: Wings yellow. Hindwing with a silver spot double-ringed in red; faint rows of fine dots in from margin.
• Can hybridize with Orange Sulphur.

Habitat

Open areas, meadows, gardens.

Adult Food

Nectar, puddling.

Larval Food

Clovers, alfalfa.

Life History

Egg: 4–7 days; Larva: 2–4 weeks; Pupa: 8–14 days; Adult: 6–10 days. Broods: N: 3; S: 5. Overwinters as larva or pupa.

Orange Sulphur
Colias eurytheme, 1⅝–2⅜″

I.D.

Medium-sized, rounded wings, orange. ABOVE: Wings orangish, bordered with black. Occasionally females are white above. BELOW: Wings orange (especially at base of forewing) to yellow. Hindwing with one or two silver spots ringed in red; row of fine dots in from margin. • Can hybridize with Clouded Sulphur.

Habitat

Open areas, meadows, gardens.

Adult Food

Nectar, puddling.

Larval Food

Alfalfa, vetches, clovers.

Life History

Egg: 4–7 days; Larva: 2–4 weeks; Pupa: 8–14 days; Adult: 6–10 days. Broods: N: 3; S: 5. Overwinters as larva or pupa.

Sleepy Orange
Eurema nicippe, 1⅜ – 1⅞″

I.D. Medium-sized, rounded wings, orange. ABOVE: Orange with black borders. BELOW: Hindwing is yellow or reddish with a faint diagonal line in center.

Habitat Wide variety of habitats.

Adult Food Nectar, puddling.

Larval Food Sennas.

Life History Egg: 4–7 days; Larva: 2–4 weeks; Pupa: 8–14 days; Adult: 6–10 days. Broods: N: 2–3; S: 3–5. Overwinters as adult.

Southern Dogface

Zerene cesonia, 1⅞ – 2½"

I.D.

Medium-sized, rounded wings, yellow. ABOVE: Forewing yellow with outline of "dog face" in edge of wing; a dark spot makes the dog's eye. BELOW: A fainter version of above.

Habitat

Open arid areas.

Adult Food

Nectar, puddling.

Larval Food

Indigo bush, prairie clover.

Life History

Egg: 4–7 days; Larva: 2–4 weeks; Pupa: 8–14 days; Adult: 6–10 days. Broods: N: 1–2; S: 3. Overwinters as adult.

Cloudless Sulphur

Phoebis sennae, 2¼–2¾"

I.D.
Medium-sized, rounded wings, yellow. Largest sulphur north of Fla. and southern Tex. Above: Male yellow; females yellow to whitish with one dark dot in each forewing. Below: Male yellow with a few dark dots; female (shown) white to yellow beneath with more extensive dots.

Habitat
Variety of open areas.

Adult Food
Nectar, puddling.

Larval Food
Sennas.

Life History
Egg: 4–7 days; Larva: 2–4 weeks; Pupa: 8–14 days; Adult: 6–10 days. Broods: N: 1; S: 3. Overwinters as adult.

Orange-barred Sulphur

Phoebis philea, 2¾–3¼″

I.D.

Medium-sized, rounded wings, yellow. One of the larger sulphurs; limited mostly to Fla. and southern Tex. ABOVE: Deep yellow with a bright orange smudge on forewing and hindwing. BELOW: Deep yellow to orange to pinkish (in female); short wavy lines on both wings.

Habitat

Parks and gardens.

Adult Food

Nectar, puddling.

Larval Food

Sennas.

Life History

Egg: 4–7 days; Larva: 2–4 weeks; Pupa: 8–14 days; Adult: 6–10 days. Broods: 1–3. Overwintering stage not known.

Large Orange Sulphur
Phoebis agarithe, 2¼–2½"

I.D.

Medium-sized, rounded wings, yellow. One of the larger sulphurs. Limited mostly to southern Fla. and southern Tex. Wanders irregularly into rest of range. ABOVE: Bright orange-yellow. BELOW: Forewing has diagonal line from tip inward; female has more extensive markings.

Habitat

Edges and clearings.

Adult Food

Nectar.

Larval Food

Woody plants of mimosa family, catclaw, blackbead.

Life History

Egg: 4–7 days; Larva: 2–4 weeks; Pupa: 8–14 days; Adult: 6–10 days. Broods: N: 1; S: 3+. Overwintering stage not known.

Gulf Fritillary
Agraulis vanillae, 2½ – 2⅞"

I.D. Medium-sized, rounded wings, dark. Long forewings. ABOVE: Deep orange with black dots. BELOW: Large, elongated, silvery dots.

Habitat Open areas, gardens, woods edges.

Adult Food Nectar, some puddling.

Larval Food Passionflowers.

Life History Egg: 4–8 days; Larva: 2–3 weeks; Pupa: 5–10 days; Adult: 2–4 weeks. Broods: N: 1; S: 4+. Overwinters as adult.

Viceroy
Limenitis archippus, 2⅝–3"

I.D.

Medium-sized, rounded wings, dark. ABOVE: Orange with black border and black wing veins. Hindwing has additional thin black horizontal bar through center. This distinguishes Viceroy from Monarch. BELOW: Similar to above.

Habitat

Edges of swamps, lakes, and rivers, gardens, parks.

Adult Food

Nectar, sap, dung, puddling.

Larval Food

Willows, aspens, cottonwoods, some fruit trees.

Life History

Egg: 4–9 days; Larva: 3–4 weeks; Pupa: 7–14 days; Adult: 6–14 days. Broods: N: 2; S: 3. Overwinters as larva.

American Lady
Vanessa virginiensis, 1¾ – 2⅛"

I.D. Medium-sized, rounded wings, dark. ABOVE: Orange with dark markings. Tips of forewings black with white dots. BELOW: Hindwing has just two large eyespots near edge.

Habitat Open sunny spots with low vegetation.

Adult Food Nectar, puddling.

Larval Food Everlasting, pussytoes, and related composites.

Life History Egg: 4–14 days; Larva: 2–4 weeks; Pupa: 7–14 days; Adult: 6–20 days. Broods: N: 1; S: 2+. Overwinters as adult.

Painted Lady
Vanessa cardui, 2–2¼"

I.D.
Medium-sized, rounded wings, dark. ABOVE: Orange with dark markings. Tips of forewings black with white dots. BELOW: Hindwing has four small eyespots near edge.

Habitat
Open sunny spots with low vegetation.

Adult Food
Nectar.

Larval Food
Thistles, other composites, hollyhocks, borages.

Life History
Egg: 4–14 days; Larva: 2–4 weeks; Pupa: 7–14 days; Adult: 6–20 days. Broods: N: 1; S: 2+. Overwinters as adult.

West Coast Lady
Vanessa annabella, 1¾ – 2"

I.D.

Medium-sized, rounded wings, dark. ABOVE: Orange with dark markings. Tips of forewings black with white dots. Hindwings orange with four small blue dots encircled with black. BELOW: Hindwing has four small eyespots near edge that blend in with rest of design.

Habitat

Roadsides, gardens, fields.

Adult Food

Nectar, dung.

Larval Food

Mallows, nettles.

Life History

Egg: 4–14 days; Larva: 2–4 weeks; Pupa: 7–14 days; Adult: 6–20 days. Broods: SW: 3+; elsewhere: 2. Overwinters as adult.

Variegated Fritillary

Euptoieta claudia, 1¾–2¼″

I.D. Medium-sized, rounded wings, dark. ABOVE: Dull orange with slightly paler band down center of forewing and hindwing. BELOW: Hindwing has pale band through center.

Habitat Fields, meadows, open sunny areas.

Adult Food Nectar.

Larval Food Violets, passion vines, and flax (in west).

Life History Egg: 10–15 days; Larva: overwinters; Pupa: 14–24 days; Adult: 2–10 weeks. Broods: N: 3; S: 3–4. Overwinters as adult in extreme south, as larva elsewhere.

Aphrodite Fritillary

Speyeria aphrodite, 2–2⅞"

I.D. Medium-sized, rounded wings, dark. ABOVE: Wings orange checkered with black; forewing often has black border and black spots on interior. BELOW: Hindwing has little or no pale band inside silver spots on trailing edge; many large silver spots on interior.

Habitat Wide variety of habitats.

Adult Food Nectar.

Larval Food Violets.

Life History Egg: 10–15 days; Larva: overwinters; Pupa: 14–24 days; Adult: 2–10 weeks. Broods: 1. Overwinters as larva.

63

Atlantis Fritillary
Speyeria atlantis, 1¾–2⅝"

I.D. Medium-sized, rounded wings, dark. ABOVE: Wings orange checkered with black; forewings have solid black border. BELOW: Hindwing has dark trailing margin bordered by silver spots and a narrow band of light brown.

Habitat Open woodlands, bogs, moist meadows.

Adult Food Nectar, sometimes dung.

Larval Food Violets.

Life History Egg: 10–15 days; Larva: overwinters; Pupa: 14–24 days; Adult: 2–10 weeks. Broods: 1. Overwinters as larva.

Meadow Fritillary
Boloria bellona, 1¼ – 1⅞"

I.D.
Medium-sized, rounded wings, dark. ABOVE: Wings orange checkered with black; pale orange with no black border. BELOW: Hindwings brown with grayish band through center; no silver spots.

Habitat
Moist open areas.

Adult Food
Nectar, dung.

Larval Food
Violets.

Life History
Egg: 5–9 days; Larva: 3–4 weeks; Pupa: 7 days; Adult: 6–14 days. Broods: E: 2–3; W: 1. Overwinters as larva.

Common Buckeye
Junonia coenia, 2 – 2½″

I.D. Medium-sized, rounded wings, dark. ABOVE: Mostly brown with large eyespots; forewing has one; hindwing has two, the upper one larger. BELOW: Forewing has large eyespot surrounded by yellow, but often hidden by overlapping hindwing.

Habitat Areas of low vegetation and open ground.

Adult Food Nectar, puddling.

Larval Food Plantains, snapdragons.

Life History Egg: 4–14 days; Larva: 2–4 weeks; Pupa: 7–14 days; Adult: 6–20 days. Broods: N: 1; S: 3+. Overwinters as adult.

White Peacock
Anartia jatrophae, 2 – 2¾"

I.D.

Medium-sized, rounded wings, dark. ABOVE: Whitish with a double row of orange crescents along trailing edge of forewing and hindwing. BELOW: Whitish with a narrow orange border.

Habitat

Edges of water areas, gardens, roadsides.

Adult Food

Nectar.

Larval Food

Water hyssop, ruellias, frogfruit.

Life History

Egg: 4–14 days; Larva: 2–4 weeks; Pupa: 7–14 days; Adult: 6–20 days. Broods: Many. Overwinters: May be active all winter.

Silver-spotted Skipper
Epargyreus clarus, 1¾ – 2⅜″

I.D. Medium-sized, rounded wings, dark. Thick-bodied. ABOVE: Brown; forewing has small geometric shapes of lighter tawny brown. BELOW: Hindwing is dark brown with angular bright white spot in the center.

Habitat Wide range of open habitats with flowers, gardens.

Adult Food Nectar, some puddling.

Larval Food Black locust, woody legumes.

Life History Egg: 4–7 days; Larva: 3–5 weeks; Pupa: 12–14 days; Adult: 10–20 days. Broods: N: 1; S: 3. Overwinters as larva or pupa.

68

Northern Cloudywing
Thorybes pylades, 1¼ – 1¾"

I.D.

Medium-sized, rounded wings, dark. Thick-bodied. ABOVE AND BELOW: Even brown color to wings; tiny, limited white spots on front edge and center of forewings.

Habitat

Woods edges, brushy fields, roadsides.

Adult Food

Nectar, puddling.

Larval Food

Legumes.

Life History

Egg: 4–7 days; Larva: 3–5 weeks; Pupa: 12–14 days; Adult: 10–20 days. Broods: N: 1; S: 2. Overwinters as larva.

Mangrove Skipper
Phocides pigmalion, 2–2½″

I.D.

Medium-sized, rounded wings, dark. Thick-bodied. ABOVE AND BELOW: Black with variable amounts of deep iridescent blue; can look completely black in some lights.

Habitat

Coastal mangroves of southern Fla.

Adult Food

Nectar.

Larval Food

Red mangrove.

Life History

Egg: 4–7 days; Larva: 3–5 weeks; Pupa: 12–14 days; Adult: 10–20 days. Broods: Many. Overwinters: May be active all winter.

Eyed Brown
Satyrodes eurydice, 1⁵⁄₈ – 2″

I.D. Medium-sized, rounded wings, dark. ABOVE: Faded brown; eyespots sometimes indistinct. BELOW: Eyespots distinct, four on forewing and six on hindwing; all are small, about equal size, and have white "pupils."

Habitat Wet areas with sedges, roadside ditches, marshes, moist meadows.

Adult Food Sap, rarely nectar.

Larval Food Sedges.

Life History Egg: 6–20 days; Larva: 3–4 weeks; Pupa: 10–16 days; Adult: 6–14 days. Broods: 1+. Overwinters as larva.

Common Wood Nymph
Cercyonis pegala, 2–2⅞"

I.D. Medium-sized, rounded wings, dark. ABOVE AND BELOW: Dark brown; forewing has two large eyespots; in coastal populations eyespots are surrounded by distinctive yellow patch.

Habitat Prairies, fields, woods edges, salt marshes.

Adult Food Plant juices, some nectar.

Larval Food Grasses.

Life History Egg: 6–20 days; Larva: 3–4 weeks; Pupa: 10–16 days; Adult: 6–14+ days. Broods: 1. Overwinters as larva.

Little Wood Satyr
Megisto cymela, 1¾ – 1⅞"

I.D.
Medium-sized, rounded wings, dark. ABOVE: Light brown; two large widely spaced eyespots on both forewing and hindwing. BELOW: Eyespots similar; sometimes a few smaller spots are around larger ones.

Habitat
Woods with grasses, fields.

Adult Food
Sap, rarely nectar.

Larval Food
Grasses.

Life History
Egg: 6–20 days; Larva: 3–4 weeks; Pupa: 10–16 days; Adult: 6–14+ days. Broods: N: 1; S: 2–3. Overwinters as larva.

Georgia Satyr
Neonympha areolata, 1½–1¾"

I.D. Medium-sized, rounded wings, dark. ABOVE: Plain brown with no eyespots. BELOW: Hindwing with five eyespots; the center three are large, elongated, with multiple blue dots in their dark centers.

Habitat Grass areas in pine woods.

Adult Food Not known.

Larval Food Grasses and sedges.

Life History Egg: 6–20 days; Larva: 3–4 weeks; Pupa: 10–16 days; Adult: 6–14+ days. Broods: N: 1; S: many. Overwinters as larva.

Hackberry Emperor
Asterocampa celtis, 1¾–2¼"

I.D. Medium-sized, rounded wings, dark. ABOVE: Forewings quite pointed; dark to light brown; white spots at tips and one to three dark eyespots along margin. BELOW: Grayish brown with many eyespots on hindwing.

Habitat Wooded areas where there are hackberry trees.

Adult Food Sap, carrion, fruit, dung, nectar.

Larval Food Hackberry.

Life History Egg: 3–9 days; Larva: 4–6 weeks; Pupa: 7–10 days; Adult: 6–14 days. Broods: N: 2; S: 2+. Overwinters as larva.

Tawny Emperor
Asterocampa clyton, 1⅞ – 2⅜″

I.D.

Medium-sized, rounded wings, dark. ABOVE: Forewings quite pointed and tawny brown; tips of forewings have orange to whitish spots and no dark eyespot. BELOW: Grayish brown with many eyespots on hindwing margin.

Habitat

Wooded streams.

Adult Food

Sap, carrion, fruit, dung, nectar.

Larval Food

Hackberry.

Life History

Egg: 3–9 days; Larva: 4–6 weeks; Pupa: 7–10 days; Adult: 6–14 days. Broods: N: 1; S: 3. Overwinters as larva.

Red Admiral
Vanessa atalanta, 1³⁄₄ – 2¹⁄₄″

I.D.

Medium-sized, rounded wings, dark. ABOVE: Dark with orange bar through center of forewings and on trailing edge of hindwings; white spots on tip of forewing. BELOW: Dark with dark pink bar on forewing.

Habitat

Open woods, meadows, gardens.

Adult Food

Sap, fruit, dung, nectar.

Larval Food

Nettles.

Life History

Egg: 4–14 days; Larva: 2–4 weeks; Pupa: 7–14 days; Adult: 6–20 days. Broods: N: 1–2; S: 2–4. Overwinters as adult.

77

Baltimore Checkerspot

Euphydryas phaeton, 1⅝–2½"

I.D.
Medium-sized, rounded wings, dark. ABOVE: Black with rows of white dots next to an orange border. BELOW: The same orange border, with more rows of white spots.

Habitat
Marshes, dry fields.

Adult Food
Nectar.

Larval Food
Turtlehead, plantains.

Life History
Egg: 14–20 days; Larva: over-winters; Pupa: 14–18 days; Adult: 6–10 days. Broods: 1. Overwinters as larva.

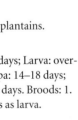

Bordered Patch
Chlosyne lacinia, 1⅝ – 1⅞"

I.D. Medium-sized, rounded wings, dark. ABOVE: Wings black with wide orange band through center. BELOW: Similar, with an additional pale narrow band near border.

Habitat Wide variety: pine or oak woods, thorn forest, gardens, hedgerows.

Adult Food Nectar; Males: dung, carrion, puddling.

Larval Food Sunflower, giant ragweed, cowpen daisy.

Life History Egg: 10–15 days; Larva: overwinters; Pupa: 14–24 days; Adult: 2–10 weeks. Broods: Several. Overwinters as larva.

Zebra
Heliconius charitonius, 3–3⅜"

I.D. Medium-sized, rounded wings, dark. Long forewings. ABOVE AND BELOW: Black with thin yellow stripes.

Habitat Moist wood edges, woodland clearings.

Adult Food Nectar, some puddling.

Larval Food Passionflowers.

Life History Egg: 4–8 days; Larva: 2–3 weeks; Pupa: 5–10 days; Adult: 1–5 months. Broods: N: 1; S: 4+. Overwinters as adult; active all winter in extreme south.

California Sister

Adelpha bredowii, 2⅞–3⅜″

I.D.

Medium-sized, rounded wings, dark. ABOVE: Black with broad white band through center of wings; orange on tips of forewings bordered by black. BELOW: Similar to above and with iridescent blue stripes at base of wings.

Habitat

Oak woods.

Adult Food

Nectar, fruit, puddling.

Larval Food

Oaks.

Life History

Egg: 4–9 days; Larva: 3–4 weeks; Pupa: 7–14 days; Adult: 6–14 days. Broods: N: 1; S: 2+. Overwinters as larva.

Lorquin's Admiral
Limenitis lorquini, 2¼ – 2¾"

I.D. Medium-sized, rounded wings, dark. ABOVE: Black with broad white band through centers of wings; orange on tips of forewings extends to wing edges. BELOW: Similar to above.

Habitat Edges of forests or tree-lined streams, hedgerows, parks.

Adult Food Nectar, puddling.

Larval Food Willows, aspens, cottonwoods, chokecherry.

Life History Egg: 4–9 days; Larva: 3–4 weeks; Pupa: 7–14 days; Adult: 6–14 days. Broods: N: 1; S: 1–2. Overwinters as larva.

Red-spotted Purple
Limenitis arthemis, 3–3⅜"

I.D.
Medium-sized, rounded wings, dark. ABOVE: Black shaded with iridescent blue increasing to brilliant blue on hindwings. BELOW: Dark with three lines of white and blue dashes and a line of large reddish dots along borders.

Habitat
Open woods, woods edges, adjacent fields.

Adult Food
Nectar, carrion, fruit, dung, sap.

Larval Food
Wild cherry, aspens, poplars.

Life History
Egg: 4–9 days; Larva: 3–4 weeks; Pupa: 7–14 days; Adult: 6–14 days. Broods: N: 2; S: 2–3. Overwinters as larva.

White Admiral
Limenitis arthemis arthemis,
2⅞–3⅛"

I.D.

Medium-sized, rounded wings, dark. ABOVE: Black with shadings of iridescent blue; broad white band through center of forewing and hindwing. ABOVE AND BELOW: Hindwings have margins with blue and white dashes and then large red dots.

Habitat

Open deciduous woods and woods edges.

Adult Food

Nectar, dung, carrion, honeydew, fruit, sap.

Larval Food

Birches, aspens, poplars.

Life History Egg: 4–9 days; Larva: 3–4 weeks; Pupa: 7–14 days; Adult: 6–14+ days. Broods: N: 1; S: 2. Overwinters as larva.

Weidemeyer's Admiral

Limenitis weidemeyerii, 2¾ – 3⅜"

I.D.

Medium-sized, rounded wings, dark. ABOVE: Black with very broad white band through center of forewing and hindwing. BELOW: Hindwing lacks any blue or white dashes along border; mostly whitish with band of orange dots on hindwing.

Habitat

Wooded glens, streamsides lined with trees.

Adult Food

Nectar, carrion, sap, puddling.

Larval Food

Willows, aspens, cottonwoods.

Life History

Egg: 4–9 days; Larva: 3–4 weeks; Pupa: 7–14 days; Adult: 6–14 days. Broods: N: 1; S: 2. Overwinters as larva.

Eastern Tailed-Blue
Everes comyntas, ¾ – 1″

I.D.
Small, with tails; one tail on each hindwing. Above: Blue. Below: Hindwing grayish with two to three orange spots by tail; numerous black spots on interior.

Habitat
Open areas with some shrubs.

Adult Food
Nectar.

Larval Food
Vetches, clovers, alfalfa, other legumes.

Life History
Egg: 3–6 days; Larva: 2–3 weeks; Pupa: 8–12 days; Adult: 4–10 days. Broods: N: 2; S: 3+. Overwinters as larva.

Western Tailed-Blue
Everes amyntula, ⅞ – 1⅛"

I.D.

Small, with tails; one tail on each hindwing. Tails are fine and sometimes break off, as in photo shown. ABOVE: Blue. BELOW: Hindwing pale gray with numerous black spots; tiny orange chevrons on margin.

Habitat

Open areas with some shrubs.

Adult Food

Nectar, puddling.

Larval Food

Vetches, milk vetches, and other legumes.

Life History

Egg: 3–6 days; Larva: 2–3 weeks; Pupa: 8–12 days; Adult: 4–10 days. Broods: E: 1; W: 1+. Overwinters as larva.

Gray Hairstreak
Strymon melinus, 1–1¼"

I.D. Small, with tails, one on each hindwing. ABOVE: Dark gray or brown with orange spot on hindwing. BELOW: Gray with two orange dots near tail; interior line of dashes composed of thin white, black, and orange lines.

Habitat Open weedy areas.

Adult Food Nectar.

Larval Food Many plants, especially legumes and mallows.

Life History Egg: 4–6 days; Larva: 3–4 weeks; Pupa: 10–20 days; Adult: 4–10 days. Broods: N: 2; S: 3+. Overwinters as pupa.

Red-banded Hairstreak
Calycopis cecrops, ¾–1"

I.D. Small, with tails; two tails on each hindwing. ABOVE: Dark brown with pale blue patches. BELOW: Grayish brown; hindwing with interior orange band bordered by thin white and black lines.

Habitat Open country, woods edges.

Adult Food Nectar, puddling.

Larval Food Detritus, especially sumac.

Life History Egg: 4–6 days; Larva: 3–4 weeks; Pupa: 10–20 days; Adult: 4–10 days. Broods: N: 2; S: 3+. Overwinters as larva.

California Hairstreak
Satyrium californica, 1–1¼″

I.D.
Small, with tails. ABOVE: Brown; yellow marks near margins. BELOW: Hindwing brownish with row of black dots through center and two large spots near tail, one orange and one blue; also a few smaller orange spots.

Habitat
Drier areas of canyons and foothills.

Adult Food
Nectar.

Larval Food
Buckbrush, antelope brush, oaks, and cherries.

Life History
Egg: 4–6 days; Larva: 3–4 weeks; Pupa: 10–20 days; Adult: 4–10 days. Broods: 1. Overwinters as egg.

Striped Hairstreak
Satyrium liparops, 1–1⅜"

I.D.

Small, with tails. ABOVE: Warm brown. BELOW: Brownish with wide, offset, slightly darker bands bordered on both sides with little white lines; blue spot near tails has orange at its interior end.

Habitat

Woodlands, brushy areas.

Adult Food

Nectar.

Larval Food

Wild cherry, blueberries, and wild plums.

Egg: 4–6 days; Larva: 3–4 weeks; Pupa: 10–20 days; Adult: 4–10 days. Broods: 1. Overwinters as egg.

Life History

91

Banded Hairstreak

Satyrium calanus, 1–1¼″

I.D.

Small, with tails. ABOVE: Black. BELOW: Grayish brown; wings crossed by faint, darker broken bands bordered on only one side by little white lines.

Habitat

Edges of woods.

Adult Food

Nectar.

Larval Food

Oaks, hickories, butternut.

Life History

Egg: 4–6 days; Larva: 3–4 weeks; Pupa: 10–20 days; Adult: 4–10 days. Broods: 1. Overwinters as egg.

Hedgerow Hairstreak
Satyrium saepium, 1–1⅛"

I.D. Small, with tails. ABOVE: Reddish brown with darker border. BELOW: Brownish and fairly plain with only prominent mark a blue dot near tails of hindwing.

Habitat Brushy areas and open woodlands.

Adult Food Nectar.

Larval Food Buckbrush, wild lilac, and mountain mahogany.

Life History Egg: 4–6 days; Larva: 3–4 weeks; Pupa: 10–20 days; Adult: 4–10 days. Broods: 1. Overwinters as egg.

Golden Hairstreak
Habrodais grunus, 1–1¼"

I.D. Small, with tails; tails short and stubby. ABOVE: Brownish with darker borders. BELOW: Brownish overall with row of fine bluish and black crescents along trailing edge of hindwing.

Habitat Forested canyons and hillsides.

Adult Food Aphid honeydew, puddling.

Larval Food Chinquapin, canyon oak, huckleberry oak, and tanbark oak.

Life History Egg: 4–6 days; Larva: 3–4 weeks; Pupa: 14 days; Adult: 4–10 days. Broods: 1. Overwinters as egg.

'Olive' Juniper Hairstreak

Callophrys gryneus gryneus, ⅞ – 1″

I.D.
Small, with tails. ABOVE: Brown with lighter orange or gold marks. BELOW: Olive green. Hindwing has white line at margin, irregular white line crossing center of wing, and two white dots nearer body.

Habitat
Old fields and other areas with red cedars.

Adult Food
Nectar.

Larval Food
Red cedars.

Life History
Egg: 4–6 days; Larva: 3–4 weeks; Pupa: 10–20 days; Adult: 4–10 days. Broods: N: 2; S: 3–4. Overwinters as pupa.

'Siva' Juniper Hairstreak
Callophrys gryneus siva, ⅞–1⅛"

I.D. Small, with tails. ABOVE: Brownish with lighter marks. BELOW: Olive green. Hindwing has white line at margin, irregular white line crossing center of wing, and no white dots nearer body.

Habitat Scrubby, arid areas with red cedars.

Adult Food Nectar.

Larval Food Junipers and creeping junipers.

Life History Egg: 4–6 days; Larva: 3–4 weeks; Pupa: 10–20 days; Adult: 4–10 days. Broods: N and W: 1; SW: 2–3. Overwinters as pupa.

Great Purple Hairstreak
Atlides halesus, 1¼ – 1½"

I.D.

Small, with tails. One of the largest hairstreaks. ABOVE: Iridescent blue. BELOW: Dark with purplish hue; red spots at bases of forewings and hindwings; orange abdomen.

Habitat

Wet woodland edges.

Adult Food

Nectar.

Larval Food

Mistletoe.

Life History

Egg: 4–6 days; Larva: 3–4 weeks; Pupa: 10–20 days; Adult: 4–10 days. Broods: N: 2–3; S: 3+. Overwinters as pupa.

97

Long-tailed Skipper

Urbanus proteus, 1½ – 2″

I.D.
Small, with tails. Long tails, thick-bodied. ABOVE: Brown with iridescent turquoise along body and base of wings. BELOW: Grayish with dark band through center of hindwing.

Habitat
Brushy areas, gardens, fields.

Adult Food
Nectar.

Larval Food
Beans and other climbing legumes.

Life History
Egg: 4–7 days; Larva: 3–5 weeks; Pupa: 12–14 days; Adult: 10–20 days. Broods: N: 1; S: 3. Overwinters as adult.

Little Yellow
Eurema lisa, 1–1½″

I.D. Small, no tails, thin-bodied. ABOVE: Forewing yellow with wide black border. BELOW: Yellow with speckled appearance; rusty spot at outer edge and two tiny black dots at base of hindwing are distinctive.

Habitat Roadsides, fields, disturbed areas.

Adult Food Nectar, puddling.

Larval Food Legumes, sennas, wild sensitive plant.

Life History Egg: 4–7 days; Larva: 2–4 weeks; Pupa: 8–14 days; Adult: 6–10 days. Broods: N: 1–2; S: 4–5. Overwinters as pupa; may be active all year.

Barred Yellow
Eurema daira, 1–1³⁄₈″

I.D.
Small, no tails, thin-bodied. ABOVE: Yellow. BELOW: Hindwing rust-colored in winter, whitish peppered with black dots in summer (shown).

Habitat
Shores, dry open sites.

Adult Food
Nectar, puddling.

Larval Food
Joint vetch, pencil flower.

Life History
Egg: 4–7 days; Larva: 2–4 weeks; Pupa: 8–14 days; Adult: 6–10 days. Broods: N: 1; S: 3+. Overwinters as adult.

Dainty Sulphur
Nathalis iole, ¾ – 1⅛″

I.D. Small, no tails, thin-bodied. ABOVE: Forewing yellow with dark on tip and trailing edge. BELOW: Forewing orange with olive-scaled tip. Hindwing yellow with variable amount of olive scaling.

Habitat Open areas such as roads, rivers, fields.

Adult Food Nectar.

Larval Food Sneezeweed, shepherd's needle.

Life History Egg: 4–7 days; Larva: 2–4 weeks; Pupa: 8–14 days; Adult: 6–10 days. Broods: N: 1; S: 5. Overwinters as adult.

Little Metalmark
Calephelis virginiensis, ⅝ – ¾"

I.D.
Small, no tails, thin-bodied. ABOVE: Similar to below. BELOW: Rusty orange with two rows of silver spots on margins of hindwings and forewings; small black dots on rest of underwings.

Habitat
Pine woods, grassy coastal plains.

Adult Food
Nectar.

Larval Food
Yellow thistle.

Life History
Egg: 10 days; Larva: 10 weeks; Pupa: 10–20 days; Adult: 6–20 days. Broods: N: 3; S: 4–5. Overwintering stage not known.

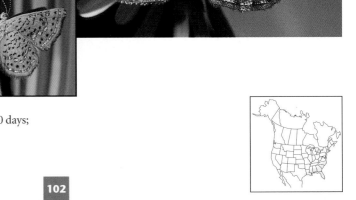

Mormon Metalmark
Apodemia mormo, ¾ – 1¼"

I.D.
Small, no tails, thin-bodied. ABOVE: Brown checkered with orange and white. BELOW: Many large white dots outlined in black. Forewing appears rusty orange at base with a darker band on margin. Hindwing is dark throughout.

Habitat
Dry areas, grasslands, shrublands, rocky washes.

Adult Food
Nectar.

Larval Food
Wild buckwheat.

Life History
Egg: 10 days; Larva: 10 weeks; Pupa: 10–20 days; Adult: 6–20 days? Broods: N: 1; S: 2+. Overwinters as larva.

Pearl Crescent
Phyciodes tharos, 1–1½"

I.D. Small, no tails, thin-bodied. ABOVE: Orange with narrow black border. ABOVE AND BELOW: Forewing has orange or pale orange — not cream-colored — band off front edge near tip.

Habitat Fields, roadsides, stream edges.

Adult Food Nectar, puddling.

Larval Food Asters.

Life History Egg: 4–10 days; Larva: 3 weeks; Pupa: 5–12 days; Adult: 4–10 days. Broods: N: 1–2; S: 5–6. Overwinters as larva.

Silvery Checkerspot
Chlosyne nycteis, 1⅜ – 1¾"

I.D. Small, no tails, thin-bodied. ABOVE: Orange with black border wider on forewing than hindwing. BELOW: Hindwing has wide pale band through center; pale at base; white crescents along border go only halfway up trailing edge.

Habitat Deciduous woods, moist meadows, stream edges.

Adult Food Nectar, puddling (in east).

Larval Food Sunflowers, asters, and other composites.

Life History Egg: 10–15 days; Larva: overwinters; Pupa: 14–24 days; Adult: 2–10 weeks. Broods: N: 1; S: 2. Overwinters as larva.

Phaon Crescent
Phyciodes phaon, ⅞–1¼″

I.D. Small, no tails, thin-bodied. ABOVE: Orange; forewing and hindwing have wide black borders. ABOVE AND BELOW: Forewing has pale creamy patch off front edge.

Habitat Open areas with low vegetation, roadsides, dunes.

Adult Food Nectar.

Larval Food Frogfruit.

Life History Egg: 4–10 days; Larva: 3 weeks; Pupa: 5–12 days; Adult: 4–10 days. Broods: N: 2; S: 3+. Overwintering stage not known.

Field Crescent
Phyciodes campestris, 1–1⅜"

I.D.

Small, no tails, thin-bodied.
ABOVE: Mostly black with several rows of orange and reddish-orange dots along borders. BELOW: Mostly orange and cream with no black dots.

Habitat

Fields, roadsides, stream edges.

Adult Food

Nectar.

Larval Food

Asters.

Life History

Egg: 4–10 days; Larva: 3 weeks; Pupa: 5–12 days; Adult: 4–10 days. Broods: N: 1–2; Plains: 2; Calif.: 3–4. Overwinters as larva.

107

Harvester
Feniseca tarquinius, 1⅛ – 1¼"

I.D. Small, no tails, thin-bodied. ABOVE: Dark orange with black blotches. BELOW: Warm brown with many white irregular circles.

Habitat Swampy areas, lake and river edges with shrubs.

Adult Food Aphid honeydew, sap, carrion, dung, puddling.

Larval Food Woolly aphids on alders, beeches.

Life History Egg: 3–4 days; Larva: 8 days; Pupa: 11 days; Adult: ?
Broods: N: 2; S: 3+. Overwinters as larva.

American Copper
Lycaena phlaeas, ⅞ – 1⅛″

I.D.

Small, no tails, thin-bodied. ABOVE: Forewings orange with dark borders and interior spots; hindwings brownish, orange band with dark spots along trailing edge. BELOW: Forewing orange with silver tip and dark dots; hindwing silver with wavy orange band near border.

Habitat

Fields, yards, pastures.

Adult Food

Nectar.

Larval Food

Sorrels, docks.

Life History

Egg: 5–7 days; Larva: 4 weeks; Pupa: 10–20 days; Adult: 4–10 days. Broods: E: 2–4; W: 1. Overwinters as larva.

Purplish Copper
Lycaena helloides, 1–1¼″

I.D.

Small, no tails, thin-bodied. ABOVE: Forewings orange (female) to purplish (male) with black spots and dark border; hindwings brownish with orange wavy line along trailing edge. BELOW: Warm brown; hindwing with reddish crescents along trailing edge.

Habitat

Variety of habitats.

Adult Food

Nectar.

Larval Food

Docks, knotweeds.

Life History

Egg: 5–7 days; Larva: 4 weeks; Pupa: 10–20 days; Adult: 4–10 days. Broods: N: 1; S: 2+. Overwinters as larva.

Coral Hairstreak
Satyrium titus, 1–1¼"

I.D.

Small, no tails, thin-bodied. ABOVE: Brown with red dots along trailing margins. BELOW: Hindwings grayish brown with row of red dots all along trailing edge.

Habitat

Open brushy areas.

Adult Food

Nectar.

Larval Food

Wild cherry, wild plum.

Egg: 4–6 days; Larva: 3–4 weeks; Pupa: 10–20 days; Adult: 4–10 days. Broods: 1. Overwinters as egg.

Life History

Eastern Pine Elfin
Callophrys niphon, ¾–1¼"

I.D.
Small, no tails, thin-bodied. ABOVE: Dark brown or tan. BELOW: Hindwing has irregular bands of darker brown bordered by thin black and white lines; gray band along trailing edge.

Habitat
Forests or overgrown fields with small pines.

Adult Food
Nectar, puddling.

Larval Food
Pitch, white, and jack pines.

Life History
Egg: 4–6 days; Larva: 3–4 weeks; Pupa: 10–20 days; Adult: 4–10 days. Broods: 1. Overwinters as pupa.

Western Pine Elfin

Callophrys eryphon, ¾–1¼"

I.D.
Small, no tails, thin-bodied. ABOVE: Dark brown or orange-brown. BELOW: Hindwing has irregular bands of darker brown bordered by thin black and inconspicuous gray lines; faint gray band inside the trailing edge.

Habitat
Pine or spruce woods.

Adult Food
Nectar, puddling.

Larval Food
Lodgepole, ponderosa, and jack pines.

Life History
Egg: 4–6 days; Larva: 3–4 weeks; Pupa: 10–20 days; Adult: 4–10 days. Broods: 1. Overwinters as pupa.

Common Ringlet
Coenonympha tullia, 1–1⅞"

I.D.

Small, no tails, thin-bodied. ABOVE: Extremely variable from gray to tan to orange-brown. Usually no markings, but sometimes a faint ring near the tip of the forewing. BELOW: Also variable. Most commonly hindwings are grayish and forewing may have a single eyespot near the tip.

Habitat

Open fields, grasslands.

Adult Food

Nectar.

Larval Food

Grasses.

Life History

Egg: 6–20 days; Larva: 3–4 weeks; Pupa: 10–16 days; Adult: 6–14+ days. Broods: N: 1; S: 2. Overwinters as larva.

Spring Azure
Celastrina ladon, ¾ – 1¼"

I.D.

Small, no tails, thin-bodied. ABOVE: Violet blue. BELOW: Pale gray with variable darker markings. Hindwing has wide darker gray band on margin.

Habitat

Brushy fields, edges of woods and wetlands.

Adult Food

Nectar, puddling.

Larval Food

Dogwood, wild cherry, meadowsweet.

Life History

Egg: 3–6 days; Larva: 2–3 weeks; Pupa: 8–12 days; Adult: 4–10 days. Broods: N: 1; S: 3. Overwinters as pupa.

Silvery Blue

Glaucopsyche lygdamus, 1–1¼″

I.D.

Small, no tails, thin-bodied. ABOVE: Male blue; female brownish. BELOW: Very pale gray with a single row of black dots ringed with white on both forewing and hindwing.

Habitat

Wide variety of habitats.

Adult Food

Nectar, puddling.

Larval Food

Lupine and other legumes.

Life History

Egg: 3–6 days; Larva: 2–3 weeks; Pupa: 8–12 days; Adult: 4–10 days. Broods: 1. Overwinters as pupa.

Acmon Blue
Plebejus acmon, ¾ – 1″

I.D.
Small, no tails, thin-bodied. ABOVE: Male blue; female brownish; both have orange bands along hindwing margins. BELOW: Very pale gray. Forewing has row of black dots on margin. Hindwing has row of orange dots on margin.

Habitat
Wide variety of habitats.

Adult Food
Nectar, puddling.

Larval Food
Attended by ants; wild buckwheat, locoweed, lupine.

Life History
Egg: 3–6 days; Larva: 2–3 weeks; Pupa: 8–12 days; Adult: 4–10 days. Broods: Many. Overwinters as larva.

Square-spotted Blue

Eupholites battoides, ¾ – 1″

I.D.

Small, no tails, thin-bodied. ABOVE: Male blue with darker margins; female brown with variable orange border on hindwing. BELOW: Pale gray with variable spotting. Hindwing has band of orange dots bordered on both sides with black dots.

Habitat

Variable.

Adult Food

Nectar, puddling.

Larval Food

Attended by ants; wild buckwheat.

Life History

Egg: 3–6 days; Larva: 2–3 weeks; Pupa: 8–12 days; Adult: 4–10 days. Broods: 1. Overwinters as pupa.

Melissa Blue
Lycaeides melissa, ⅞ – 1¼"

I.D. Small, no tails, thin-bodied. ABOVE: Male blue; female brown with orange margins. BELOW: Row of orange dots along margins of forewing and hindwing.

Habitat Pine barrens, lake dunes, prairies, open fields.

Adult Food Nectar, puddling.

Larval Food Attended by ants; lupine, other legumes.

Life History Egg: 3–6 days; Larva: 2–3 weeks; Pupa: 8–12 days; Adult: 4–10 days. Broods: N: 2; S and W: 3. Overwinters as egg and young larva.

Western Pygmy-Blue

Brephidium exile, ³⁄₈ – ³⁄₄″

I.D.
Small, no tails, thin-bodied. Tiny. ABOVE: Wings brown with blue bases and white fringe. BELOW: Forewing tawny brown on outer half, gray on inner half. Hindwing has four large black dots on margin and a few smaller ones.

Habitat
Deserts, sandy coasts, and other alkaline areas.

Adult Food
Nectar.

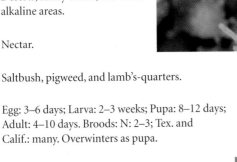

Larval Food
Saltbush, pigweed, and lamb's-quarters.

Life History
Egg: 3–6 days; Larva: 2–3 weeks; Pupa: 8–12 days; Adult: 4–10 days. Broods: N: 2–3; Tex. and Calif.: many. Overwinters as pupa.

Eastern Pygmy-Blue

Brephidium isophthalma, ½ – ¾"

I.D.

Small, no tails, thin-bodied. Tiny. ABOVE: Brown or reddish brown. BELOW: Forewing brown. Hindwing has four large black dots on margin and a few smaller ones.

Habitat

Saltwater coastal areas from S.C. to east Tex.

Adult Food

Nectar.

Larval Food

Glassworts, saltworts.

Life History

Egg: 3–6 days; Larva: 2–3 weeks; Pupa: 8–12 days; Adult: 4–10 days. Broods: N: 1–3; S: 3+. Overwinters as pupa.

Marine Blue
Leptotes marina, ⅝ – 1″

I.D.
Small, no tails, thin-bodied.
ABOVE: Purple to violet; female has brown on wing margins.
BELOW: Gray with numerous wavy bands of white lines; two dark spots on margin of hindwing.

Habitat
Mesquite scrub, variety of open areas including gardens.

Adult Food
Nectar, puddling.

Larval Food
Leadwort and a wide variety of legumes.

Life History
Egg: 3–6 days; Larva: 2–3 weeks; Pupa: 8–12 days; Adult: 4–10 days. Broods: N: ?; Calif. and Tex.: 3+. Overwintering stage not known.

Common Checkered-Skipper
Pyrgus communis, ¾–1¼"

I.D.

Small, no tails, thick-bodied.
ABOVE: Black-and-white-checkered pattern; row of tiny dots along trailing edge of wings. Male has bluish body; female has black body.
BELOW: Light with tan blotches.

Habitat

Sunny areas of low vegetation and some bare earth, gardens, fields, roadsides.

Adult Food

Nectar, puddling.

Larval Food

Mallows.

Life History

Egg: 4–7 days; Larva: 3–5 weeks; Pupa: 12–14 days; Adult: 10–20 days. Broods: N: 2; S: 3. Overwinters as larva.

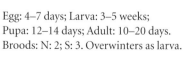

Least Skipper
Ancyloxypha numitor, ¾ – 1"

I.D.
Small, no tails, thick-bodied. ABOVE: Forewing mostly black; hindwing black with an orange center. BELOW: All orange.

Habitat
Moist open areas, meadows, marshes, old fields.

Adult Food
Nectar.

Larval Food
Variety of grasses.

Life History
Egg: 4–7 days; Larva: 3–5 weeks; Pupa: 12–14 days; Adult: 10–20 days. Broods: N: 3; S: 3–4. Overwinters as larva.

European Skipper
Thymelicus lineola, ¾–1″

I.D.
Small, no tails, thick-bodied.
ABOVE: Wings mostly orange with an even dark border.
BELOW: Wings all orange.

Habitat
Meadows, fields, other grassy areas.

Adult Food
Nectar.

Larval Food
Grasses, especially timothy.

Life History
Egg: 4–7 days; Larva: 3–5 weeks; Pupa: 12–14 days; Adult: 10–20 days. Broods: 1. Overwinters as egg.

Fiery Skipper
Hylephila phyleus, 1–1¼″

I.D. Small, no tails, thick-bodied. ABOVE: Wings orange with sharply wavy dark border. BELOW: Orange with small dark dots.

Habitat Lawns, roadsides, gardens.

Adult Food Nectar.

Larval Food Grasses, including crabgrasses.

Life History Egg: 4–7 days; Larva: 3–5 weeks; Pupa: 12–14 days; Adult: 10–20 days. Broods: N: 1; S: 3–5. Overwintering stage not known.